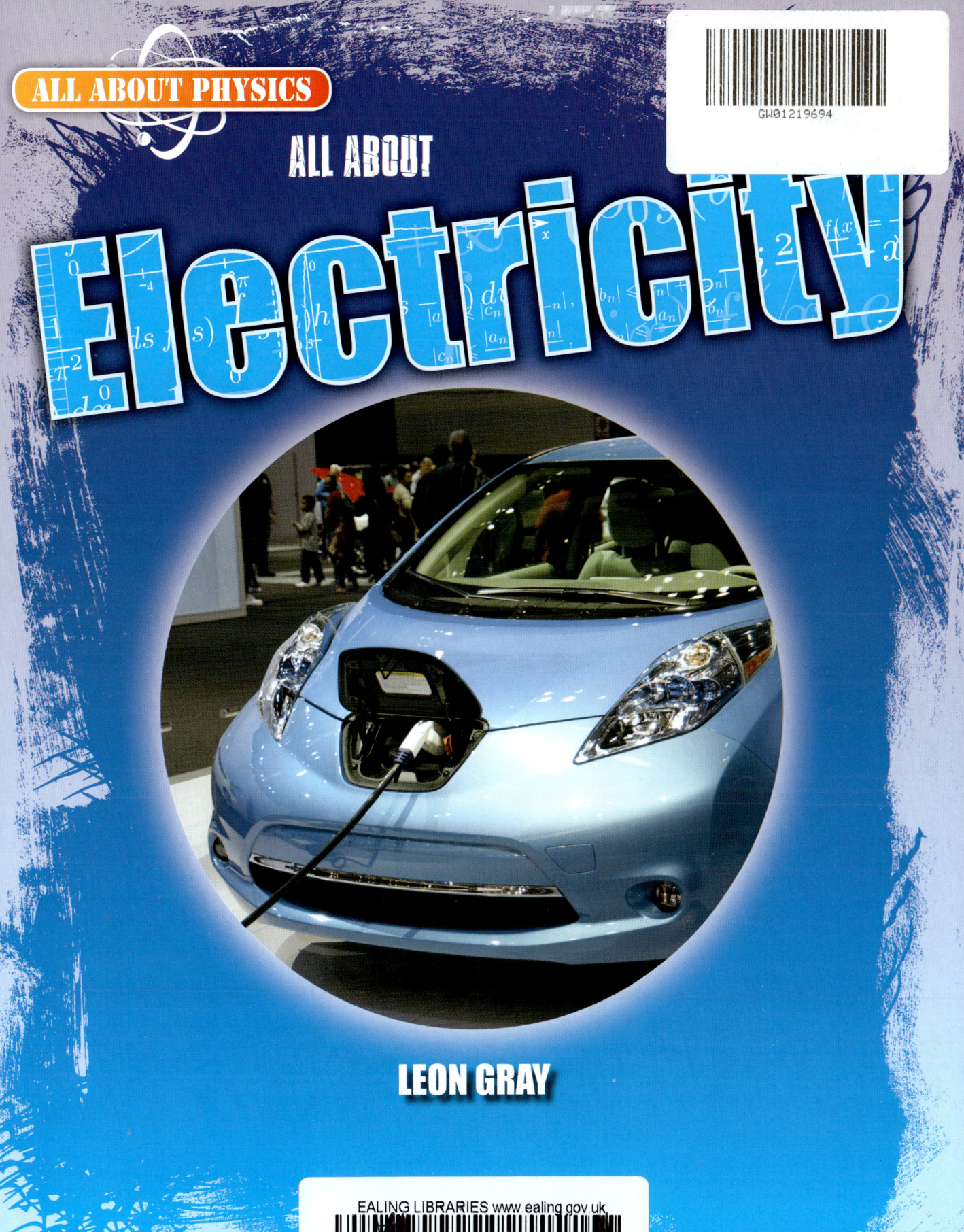

ALL ABOUT PHYSICS

ALL ABOUT Electricity

LEON GRAY

Raintree is an imprint of Capstone Global Library Limited, a company incorporated in England and Wales having its registered office at 264 Banbury Road, Oxford, OX2 7DY – Registered company number: 6695582

www.raintree.co.uk
myorders@raintree.co.uk

Text © Capstone Global Library Limited 2020
The moral rights of the proprietor have been asserted.

All rights reserved. No part of this publication may be reproduced in any form or by any means (including photocopying or storing it in any medium by electronic means and whether or not transiently or incidentally to some other use of this publication) without the written permission of the copyright owner, except in accordance with the provisions of the Copyright, Designs and Patents Act 1988 or under the terms of a licence issued by the Copyright Licensing Agency, Barnard's Inn, 86 Fetter Lane, London, EC4A 1EN (www.cla.co.uk). Applications for the copyright owner's written permission should be addressed to the publisher.

Original illustrations © Capstone Global Library Limited 2020
Originated by Capstone Global Library Ltd
Printed and bound in India

ISBN 978 1 4747 7716 2 (hardback)
ISBN 978 1 4747 7724 7 (paperback)

British Library Cataloguing in Publication Data
A full catalogue record for this book is available from the British Library.

Acknowledgements
We would like to thank the following for permission to reproduce photographs:
Cover: Shutterstock: Gui Jun Peng. Inside: Shutterstock: a45411, Againstar 22, Ambient Ideas 17, Ambrophoto 44, Anch 40, Atm2003 42, Juan Camilo Bernal 1, 35, Rob Byron 39, Martin Capek 33, DeepGreen 27, Dragon Images 41, Ensuper 21, Everett Collection 38, Gelpi 31, Igor Golovniov 14, Gst 16, Janne Hamalainen 25, Mark Herreid 8, Tony Hunt 9, Jcjgphotography 32, J.D.S 37, Karelnoppe 4t, Georgios Kollidas 29, Konstantin L 5, Alexey Malashkevich 45, Georgy Markov 24, Marzolino 26, MasterPhoto 23, MaxyM 4b, Morphart Creation 15, 20, Nicku 19, Hein Nouwens 30, Anna Omelchenko 2, 6, Tom Reichner 18, SeDmi 36, Sergemi 34, Rustam Shanov 12, Sirtravelalot 10, Tamapapat 43, Vvoe 7, Worradirek 28; Wikimedia Commons: Le Roy C. Cooley 13.

Every effort has been made to contact copyright holders of material reproduced in this book. Any omissions will be rectified in subsequent printings if notice is given to the publisher.

All the internet addresses (URLs) given in this book were valid at the time of going to press. However, due to the dynamic nature of the internet, some addresses may have changed, or sites may have changed or ceased to exist since publication. While the author and publisher regret any inconvenience this may cause readers, no responsibility for any such changes can be accepted by either the author or the publisher

Contents

- 4   Electricity
- 6   Chapter One   What is electricity?
- 12   Chapter Two   Electric charge
- 18   Chapter Three   Electric circuits
- 28   Chapter Four   Electricity and magnetism
- 36   Chapter Five   Using electricity
- 44   The future of electricity
- 46   Glossary
- 47   Find out more
- 48   Index

Electricity

Electricity is one of the most powerful forces of nature. Look up at the sky the next time there is a thunderstorm and a bolt of lightning shoots across the sky, and you will see just how powerful electricity can be. It is only recently that people have been able to use electricity as a source of energy.

Electricity provides the power for many devices, from our mobile phones to our personal music players.

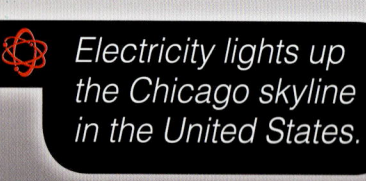

Electricity lights up the Chicago skyline in the United States.

A source of energy

Electricity is the invisible force that gives us the energy to light and heat our homes. It also helps us to power machines such as computers. When you flick a switch to make something work, it probably runs on electricity.

Electric power

Long ago, people lit fires to provide heat and light in their homes and to cook their food. There were no electric machines, so people had to do everything by hand. Things changed when scientists discovered how to use electricity as a source of energy. Today, all we have to do is plug something in, flick a switch and the energy is there.

This tram is powered by electricity that flows through overhead cables.

SUPER SCIENCE FACT

Electricity is incredibly useful but it can also be very dangerous. In fact, the electricity in our homes can be deadly. You should never push things into electrical sockets or unscrew electrical appliances. The electricity in overhead power cables and train tracks is even more dangerous, so stay far away from them.

Chapter One
What is electricity?

Electricity is a form of energy that has been around since the beginning of the universe. People use electricity for light and heat, and to power machines and vehicles. There is even electricity inside our bodies!

Lightning strikes

Lightning is an amazing example of the power of electricity. When electrical charge builds up inside clouds during a thunderstorm, we see this as lightning. The storm whips up violent swirls of air, smashing raindrops and ice crystals into each other. These particles then become electrically charged because of the force of the collisions.

Lightning occurs when static electricity builds up inside clouds and then surges through the sky towards the ground.

Electrical discharge

More and more electrical charge builds up inside the cloud until it becomes too much. The electricity then discharges (shoots) towards the ground as brilliant flashes of heat and light – the lightning you see in the sky. The lightning is so powerful that it also makes a rumbling sound – the thunder you hear during a storm.

Static electricity

Lightning is a type of electricity called static electricity (see Chapter Two). It occurs when two objects rub against each other or smash into each other, in the case of a thunderstorm. You can make static electricity by rubbing a balloon against your hair. The static electricity makes your hair stick to the balloon.

SUPER SCIENCE FACT

Lightning is very dangerous. It can set trees on fire, destroy buildings and even kill people. In the UK, 30 to 60 people are struck by lightning every year. On average, three of these people die from their injuries.

Metal lightning rods protect tall buildings from lightning bolts by conducting the powerful electricity to the ground.

Life force

Without electricity, we would not survive. Electrical signals move through our bodies. These signals make it possible for us to think, move and make sense of the world.

Brain power

Our brain is the control centre for the electrical signals that travel through our bodies. Nerves carry these signals to different parts of the body. There are more than 100 billion nerve cells, called neurons, in the brain. Every second, billions of tiny electrical signals whizz between the neurons, controlling everything we do.

Electrical senses

We can read because light rays pass into our eyes and change into electrical signals. The signals travel along nerves that lead to the brain. There, the signals are changed into images we can see.

When you touch something hot, sensory cells in your skin change the heat sensation into electrical signals. These signals travel along nerves to the brain. The brain then sends electrical signals to your arm muscles to tell them to move your hand.

Your brain works using electricity. Nerves send tiny pulses of electricity to your brain, helping you to make sense of the world.

Speedy nerves

The electrical signals in your body travel very quickly. When you touch something hot, the sensory cells in your skin send the information to your brain at more than 240 kilometres (150 miles) per hour. The brain sends messages back to your arm muscles at more than 320 kilometres (200 miles) per hour. The signals tell you to move your hand away quickly to avoid getting burned.

SUPER SCIENCE FACT

Some animals use electricity to sense the world around them. Sharks have special cells on their bodies that can pick up tiny electrical signals created as fish swim through the water.

Sharks hunt by detecting the electrical signals given off by prey.

Electricity around us

A few hundred years ago, no one knew that electricity existed. Today, electricity is all around us. We rely on electricity to light up our streets, heat our homes and to power many different machines and vehicles.

Electricity makes household jobs, such as ironing, easier and quicker.

Using electricity

We live in an age of electricity. We use it all the time and for many different things. Every time you flick on a light switch, you are using electricity. We need electricity to cook our food and keep it cool. Electricity provides us with energy to heat up our homes. Without electricity, our radios, televisions and other electronic devices simply would not work.

Moving with electricity

Electricity makes our lives easier in many other ways, too. Without it, we would not have electric-powered vehicles such as trains and trams. Even vehicles that run on petrol would not work, because electricity is needed to start and control their engines.

Connecting people

Electricity has revolutionized the way people speak to one another. In the past, people used telegraphs and telephones to communicate over long distances. These devices sent messages as electrical signals along telephone wires and, later, by radio. Today, electricity provides the power for computers and mobile phones, connecting people via blogs, chat rooms and email.

Pylons carry electricity from power stations to your home.

LIFE WITHOUT ELECTRICITY

Imagine what life was like before electricity. As recently as the early 1900s, people still lit candles for light and cooked on wood-burning stoves. They did not have vacuum cleaners or washing machines, so they swept the floor with brushes and washed clothes by hand.

Chapter Two
Electric charge

Static electricity can make our hair stand on end!

Over time, scientists came up with ideas about electricity, but no one could really explain how it worked. It was not until scientists discovered the structure of the atom that people began to understand electricity.

Amber and the ancient Greeks

The ancient Greeks were the first to study the effects of electricity to try to understand it. They rubbed amber (a fossil form of tree resin) with wool or fur, and noticed that light objects, such as feathers and leaves, then stuck to the amber.

Experiments with electricity

The first person to experiment with electricity was an English scientist called William Gilbert. He rubbed other objects, such as wax and glass, with cloth and fur, and found they also attracted light objects. Gilbert named these objects "electrics" after the Greek *elektron*, which means "amber". Over the next 200 years, many scientists experimented with electricity. They built machines that created sparks of electricity by rubbing objects together.

Benjamin Franklin was lucky to survive a lightning strike when he flew his kite during a thunderstorm.

SUPER SCIENCE FACT

In 1752, American scientist Benjamin Franklin tied a metal key to the end of a kite string and flew the kite in a thunderstorm. When he touched the key, Franklin felt a powerful electric shock pass through his body. Franklin nearly died, but he proved that lightning was a form of electricity.

Collecting and detecting

Early scientists did not have batteries and electrical switches to experiment with. Instead, they came up with inventions to collect and store electrical charge.

Dangerous experiments
When an experiment with lightning killed Russian scientist Georg Richmann, scientists decided to look for a safer way to collect and store electricity.

Collecting charge
In the 1800s, scientists found a way of creating and storing electrical charge. They built machines to create sparks of electricity. One of the most successful was the Wimshurst machine, named after its English inventor, James Wimshurst. This machine created sparks of electricity between two glass discs and metal combs that pointed to the discs.

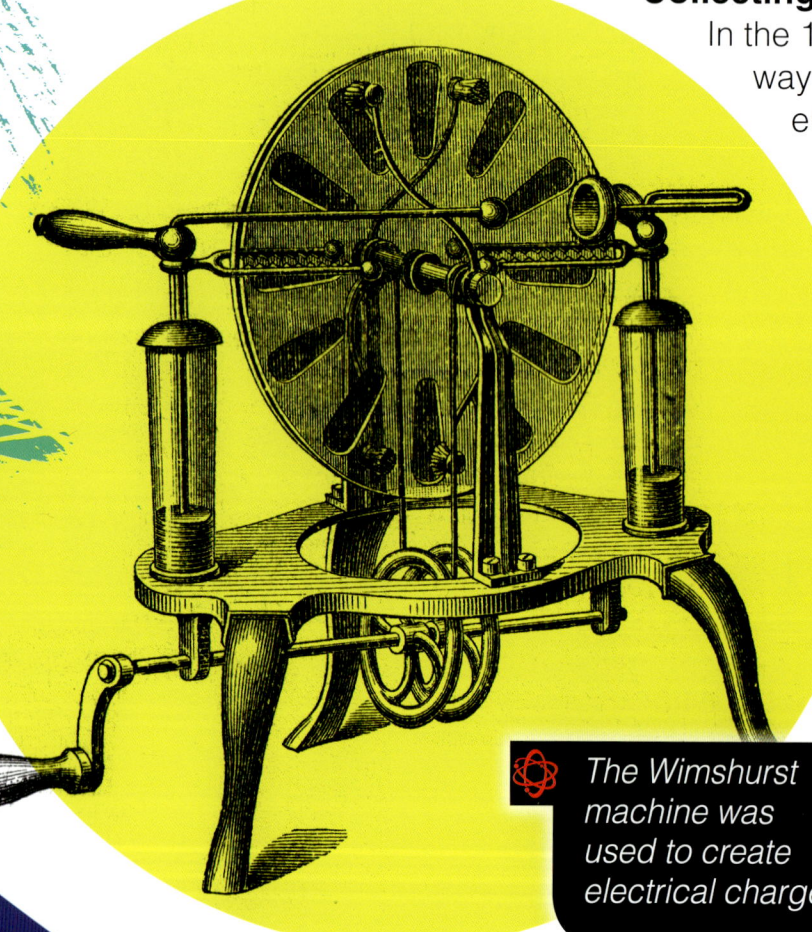

The Wimshurst machine was used to create electrical charge.

Storing electricity

Scientists then managed to store the electrical charge produced by the Wimshurst machine in a Leyden jar. This was a glass jar lined with metal foil. The electrical charge built up in the jar and could be used when it was needed. To get the electricity in the jar, scientists held a discharger rod near a metal ball at the top of the jar. The Leyden jar was useful but unreliable, because it quickly lost its charge. Scientists needed a reliable source of electricity to carry out their experiments.

SUPER SCIENCE FACT

In the 1930s, an American scientist called Robert Van de Graaff built a machine that could store huge amounts of electrical energy. The machine, called a Van de Graaff generator, relied on friction to charge up a hollow, metal sphere.

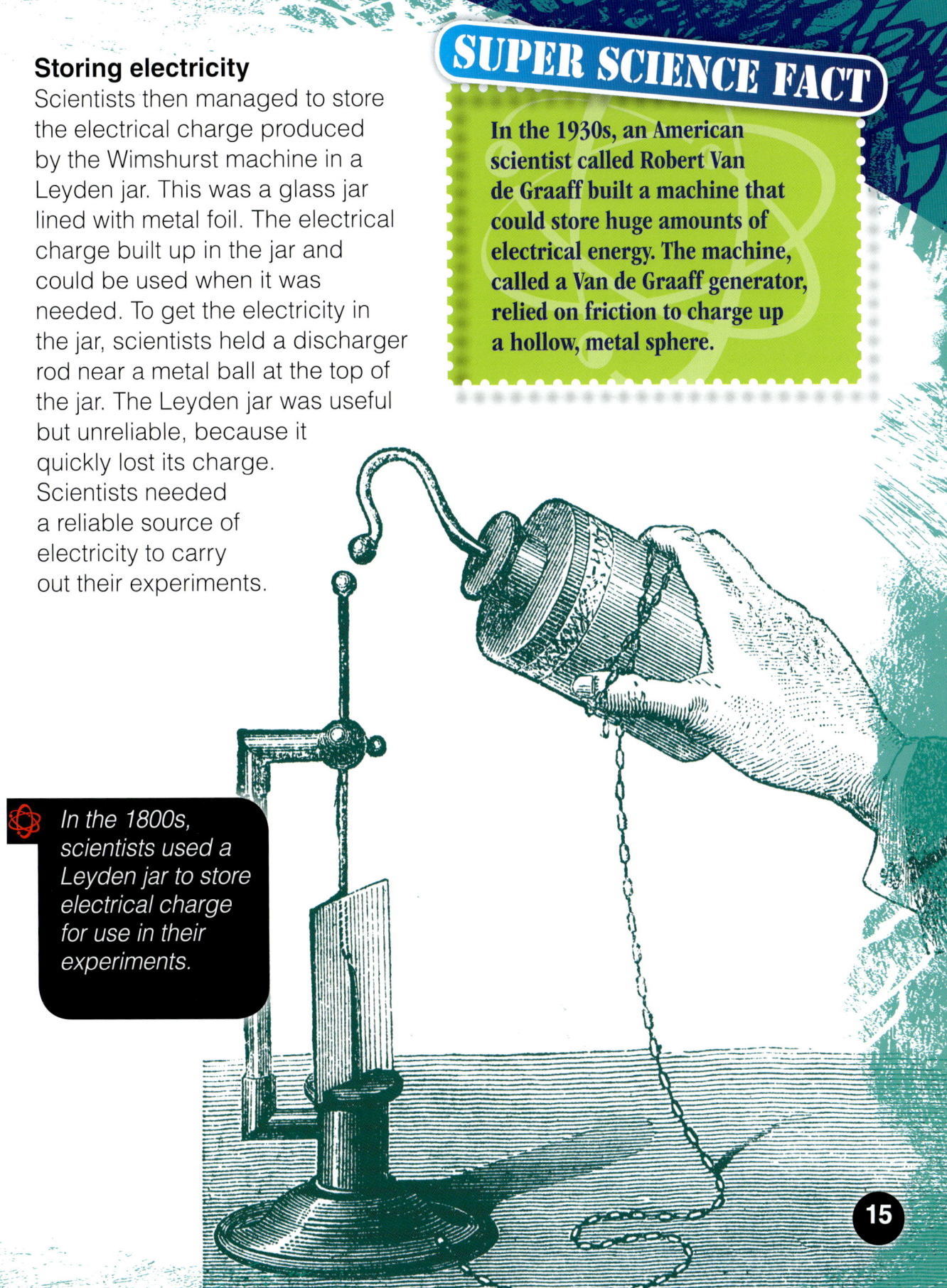

In the 1800s, scientists used a Leyden jar to store electrical charge for use in their experiments.

Inside the atom

After scientists discovered the structure of the atom at the end of the 1800s, they found that everything to do with electricity is caused by tiny charged particles inside atoms.

Protons, neutrons and electrons
Everything in the universe is made up of incredibly small particles called atoms. Atoms consist of even smaller particles called protons, neutrons and electrons. The protons and neutrons gather together in the centre of the atom in the nucleus.

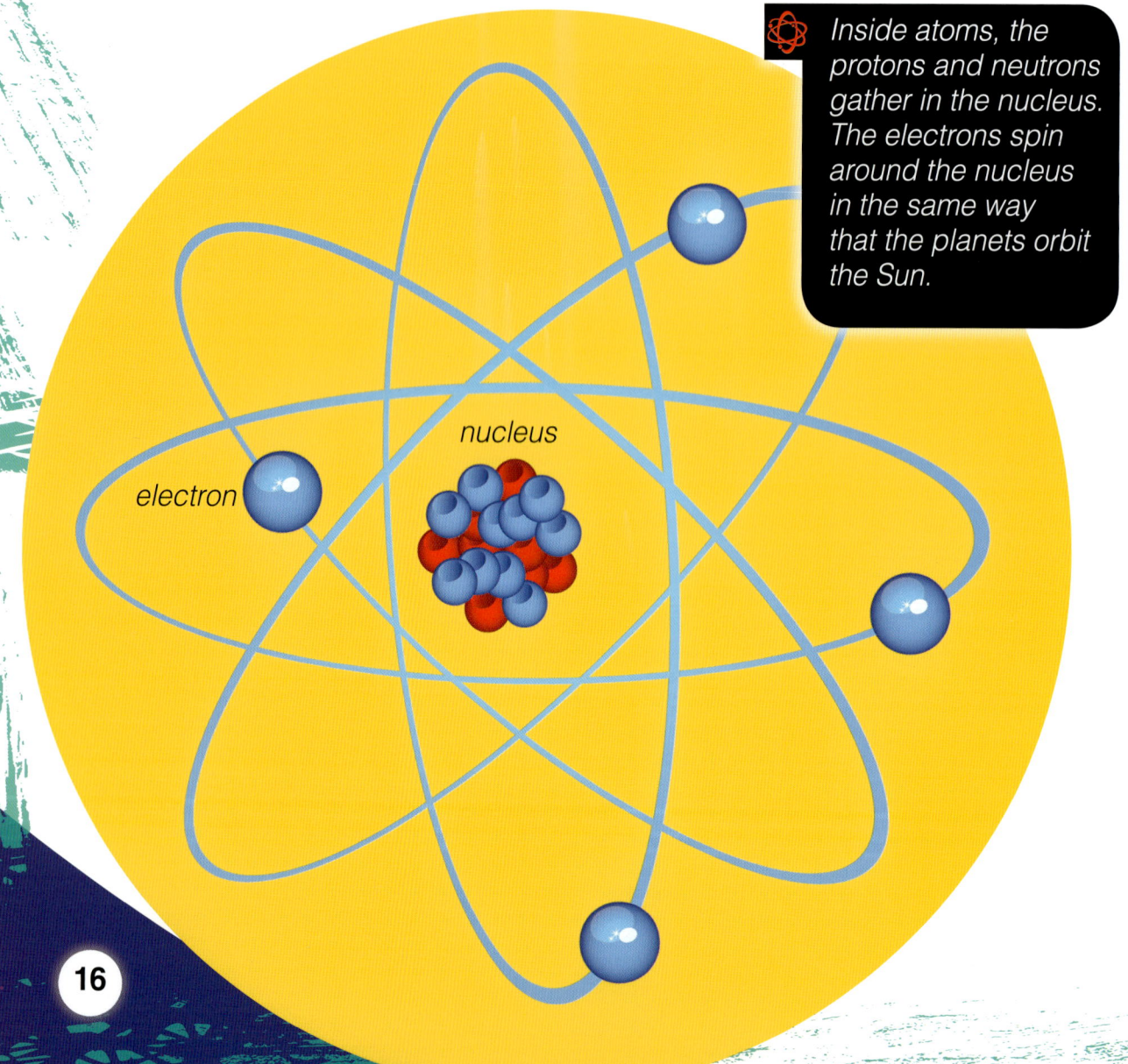

Inside atoms, the protons and neutrons gather in the nucleus. The electrons spin around the nucleus in the same way that the planets orbit the Sun.

nucleus

electron

Electric charges

Electrons and protons are charged particles, which means they carry bundles of electrical energy. Protons have a positive charge, while electrons are negatively charged. Neutrons have no electrical charge. Atoms have an equal number of positive protons and negative electrons so the atom is electrically neutral.

Charged objects

Inside an atom, the protons are tightly bound in the nucleus, but the electrons are free to move around. When an object gains electrons, it becomes negatively charged. Similarly, when an object loses electrons, it becomes positively charged.

Electricity

You can charge some objects by rubbing them together. This transfers electrons from one object to the other, and makes one positive and one negative. This is called static electricity because the electricity stays in one place. Another type of electricity is current electricity. This occurs when electrical charges move from one place to another.

From tiny insects to vast planets, everything is made up of atoms.

LIFE WITHOUT ATOMS

Atoms make up everything around you, from the air you breathe to the food you eat, and your body. In fact, without atoms there would be nothing in the world or even the universe.

Chapter Three
Electric circuits

In the late 1800s, an experiment with a frog's leg led to the invention of the battery. This provided scientists with a reliable source of current electricity. It also made it much easier for them to experiment with electricity and to understand how it works.

The nerves inside the body of a frog carry tiny electrical pulses. Scientist Luigi Galvani accidentally discovered this "animal electricity" while dissecting a frog.

Animal electricity

In the 1770s, Italian biologist Luigi Galvani cut open a frog to study the inside of its body. Galvani's metal knife accidentally touched a nerve in the dead frog's leg, and the leg twitched. Galvani thought that "animal electricity" was making the frog's leg move.

Volta's pile

Another Italian scientist, Alessandro Volta, did not agree with Galvani's "animal electricity". Volta realized the electricity was coming from the metal knife rather than the body of the frog.

Volta proved his point by using metals to build the first battery, called the Voltaic pile. He stacked copper and zinc discs into a huge pile, one on top of the other. He separated each metal disc with cardboard discs soaked in salt water. When he touched each end of the pile, Volta felt an electric shock.

SUPER SCIENCE FACT

In the Voltaic pile, the copper discs lose electrons to the moist cardboard. The zinc discs gain these electrons from the moist cardboard. The movement of electrons from the copper to the zinc creates the current Volta felt as an electric shock.

Alessandro Volta invented the first battery, called the Voltaic pile, in 1800.

Electric cells

Volta's invention transformed the study of electricity. As scientists improved on Volta's battery design, they found that they could produce a reliable source of electricity for their experiments.

Electric cells

The smallest unit of a battery that produces electricity is called an electric cell. One electric cell of the Voltaic pile consisted of one copper disc, one zinc disc and one cardboard disc soaked in salt water. The metal discs are called electrodes, and the liquid between them is called the electrolyte. Volta piled up lots of cells to make his battery because this created more electricity.

Daniell's cell

In the early 1800s, John Frederic Daniell made an electric cell that used copper and zinc as the electrodes. Daniell put the copper electrode in a chemical solution called copper sulphate. He put the zinc electrode in sulphuric acid. Daniell's simple cell provided a more reliable source of electricity than the Voltaic pile.

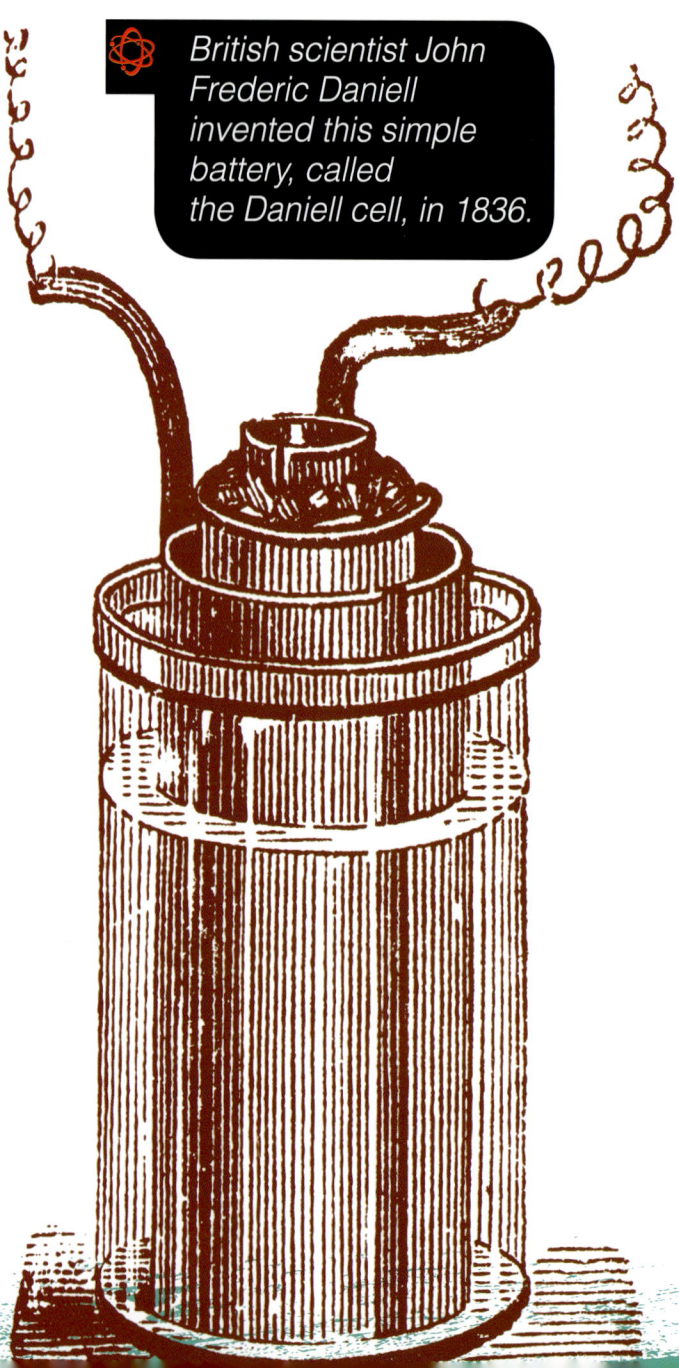

British scientist John Frederic Daniell invented this simple battery, called the Daniell cell, in 1836.

The dry cell

In the mid-1900s, French scientist Georges Leclanché made a battery that used zinc and carbon as the electrodes. He used ammonium chloride as the electrolyte. Leclanché's battery became popular because it did not contain dangerous acids. Eventually, scientists made the electrolyte into a "dry" paste. This lead to the batteries we use today.

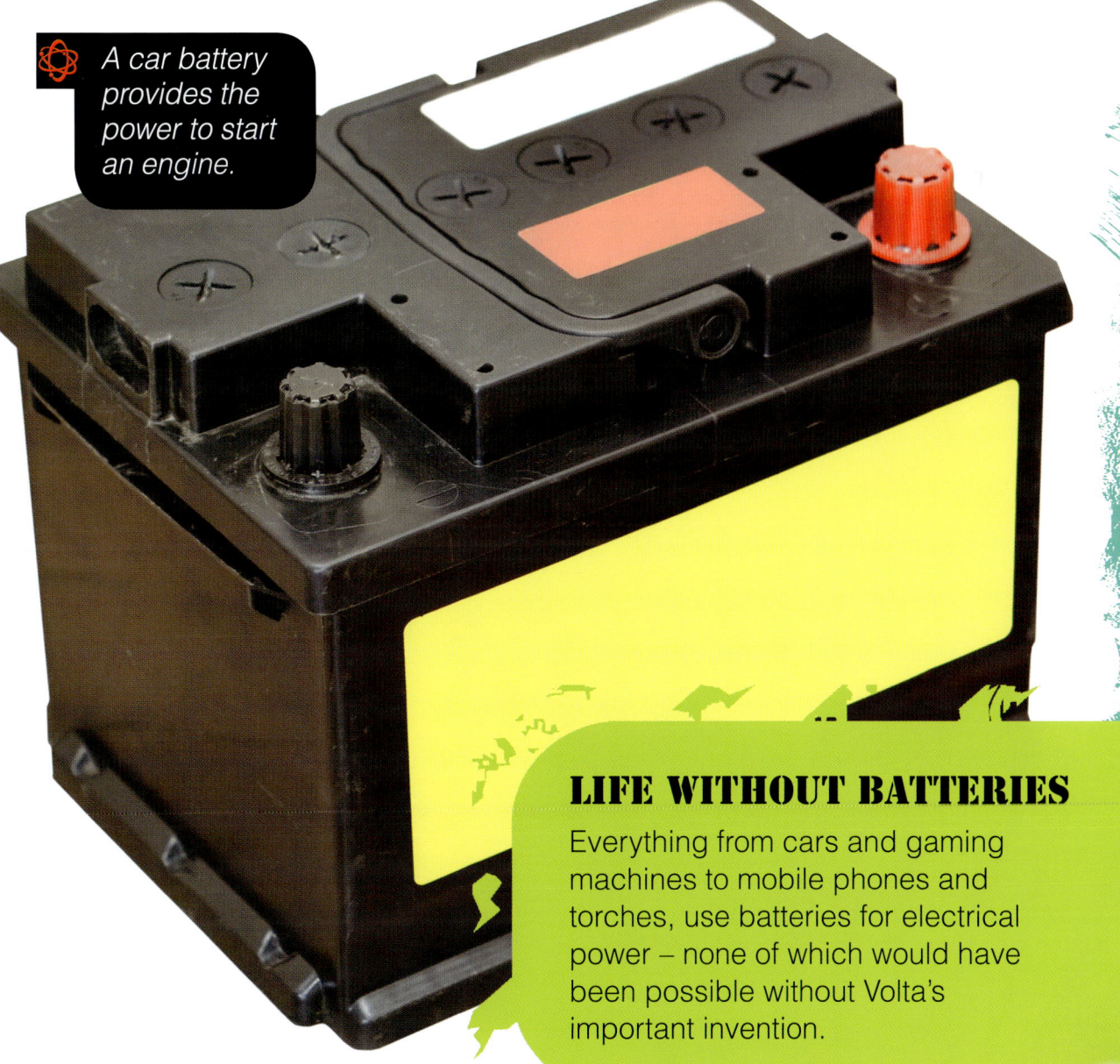

A car battery provides the power to start an engine.

LIFE WITHOUT BATTERIES

Everything from cars and gaming machines to mobile phones and torches, use batteries for electrical power – none of which would have been possible without Volta's important invention.

Conductors and insulators

As scientists experimented with batteries, they found out more about electricity. One of the first things they learned was that some materials allowed electricity to pass through them, while others did not.

Insulators
Electricity is the movement of electrons through a substance. In most materials, the electrons are tightly bound to the atoms and they do not conduct electricity very well. They are called insulators. Most plastics are good insulators. They are used to cover electrical wires and plugs to prevent people from getting electric shocks.

The electricity in a circuit passes through thin metal conducting wires.

Conductors

In other materials, some electrons are free from their atoms and can move around. These electrons carry electrical energy from one point to another. These materials are called conductors. Metals such as copper and zinc are good conductors because they contain lots of free electrons that move around.

Completing a circuit

When a conductor is connected to a battery to complete a circuit, all the electrons move in the same direction. This creates a movement of electricity called an electric current. The battery is the driving force (voltage), that pushes the electrons around the circuit.

Plugs and electric sockets are made from plastic to protect people from shocks.

SUPER SCIENCE FACT

When electrons move through a circuit, they always move from the negative electrode, which gives up electrons, to the positive electrode, which gains the electrons. This is because opposite charges attract, and like charges repel.

Resistors

When electrons move through a conductor they sometimes bump into the atoms that make up the material. The electrons slow down, which reduces the electric current. This is called resistance.

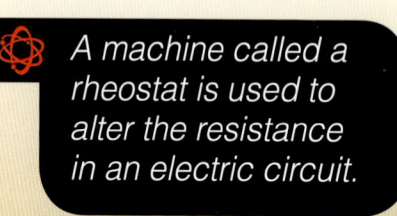

A machine called a rheostat is used to alter the resistance in an electric circuit.

Georg Ohm

The first person to study resistance was a German scientist called Georg Ohm. He found that every material has some resistance to an electric current – even the best metal conductors. Ohm experimented with different conductors and found a relationship between the resistance, current and voltage in an electric circuit.

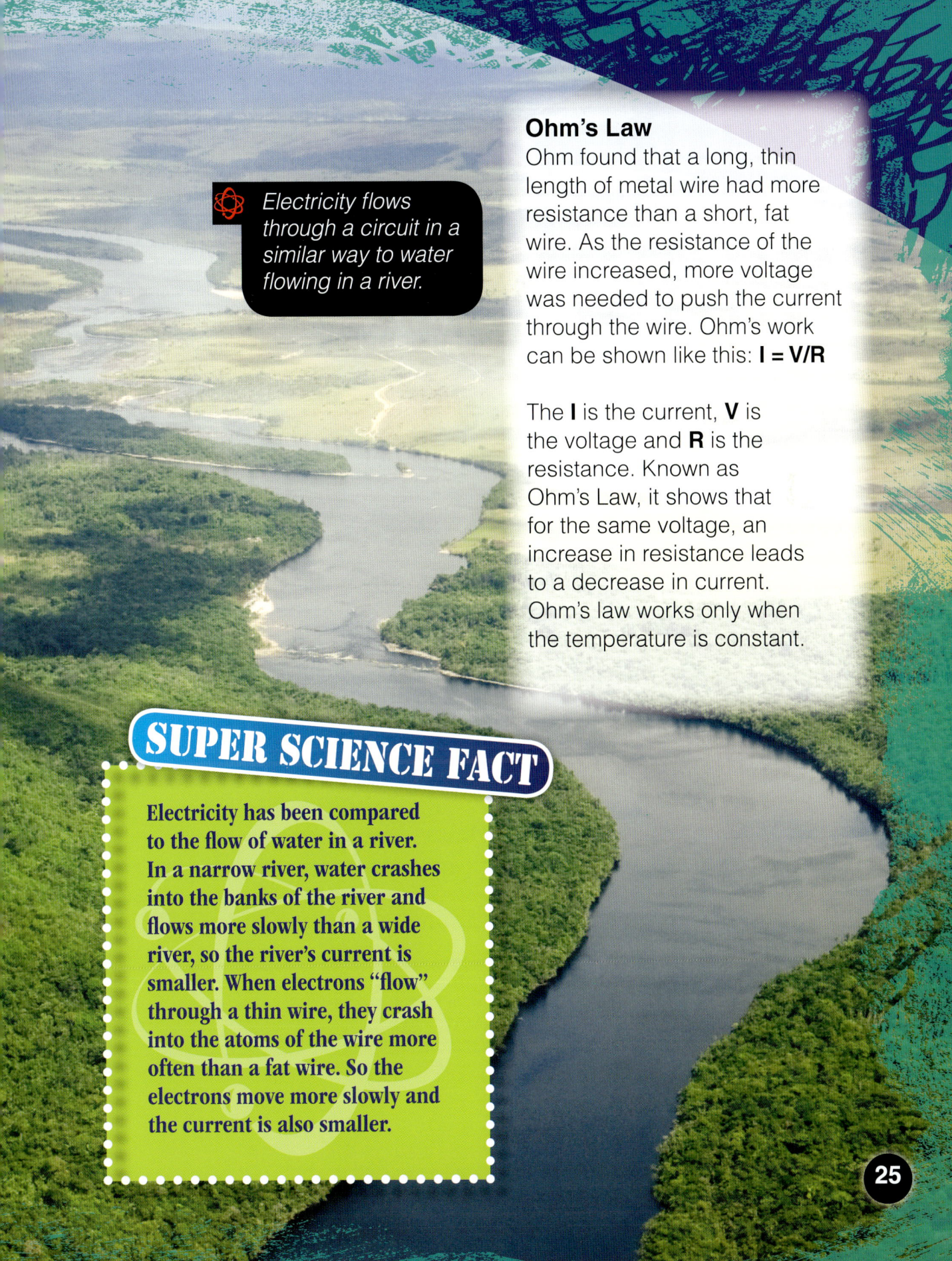

Electricity flows through a circuit in a similar way to water flowing in a river.

Ohm's Law

Ohm found that a long, thin length of metal wire had more resistance than a short, fat wire. As the resistance of the wire increased, more voltage was needed to push the current through the wire. Ohm's work can be shown like this: $I = V/R$

The **I** is the current, **V** is the voltage and **R** is the resistance. Known as Ohm's Law, it shows that for the same voltage, an increase in resistance leads to a decrease in current. Ohm's law works only when the temperature is constant.

SUPER SCIENCE FACT

Electricity has been compared to the flow of water in a river. In a narrow river, water crashes into the banks of the river and flows more slowly than a wide river, so the river's current is smaller. When electrons "flow" through a thin wire, they crash into the atoms of the wire more often than a fat wire. So the electrons move more slowly and the current is also smaller.

Electrolysis

Soon after Volta invented his Voltaic pile, British scientist William Nicholson made his own version of the battery. He used it to pass an electric current through a bowl of water. Nicholson noticed bubbles of gas appearing at each electrode. He had discovered electrolysis.

Scientists in the 1800s used simple equipment to carry out experiments with electrolysis.

Nicholson's work

When Nicholson passed electricity through water, a chemical reaction occurred. Water consists of the elements hydrogen and oxygen. Electricity had split each water molecule into its two elements. So bubbles of oxygen gas appeared at one electrode, and bubbles of hydrogen gas appeared at the other electrode.

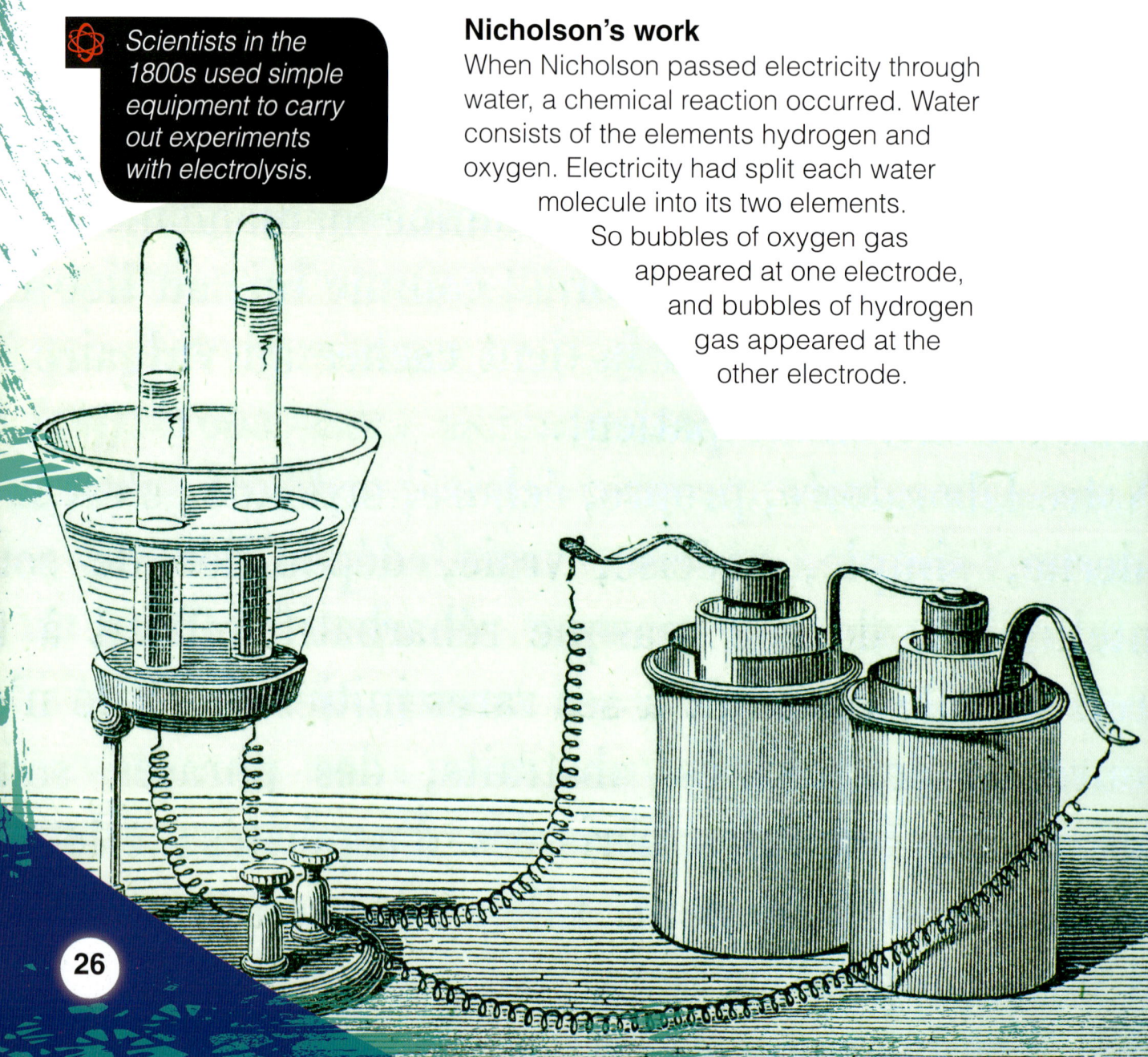

Electrolysis in action

Britain's Humphry Davy realized the importance of electrolysis. He used it to make pure potassium, and later sodium, for the first time. Potassium does not exist naturally as a pure metal – it is so reactive that it is always found combined with other elements.

Potash

One common potassium compound is potash. Potash is potassium mixed with carbon and oxygen. When Davy passed electricity through molten potash, he found that potassium metal collected at the negative electrode.

Car manufacturers use electrolysis to coat steel body parts with a layer of zinc to prevent rusting.

LIFE WITHOUT ELECTROLYSIS

Without electrolysis, cars would very quickly rust and fall apart. Most car bodies are made from steel, which rusts when it gets wet. So car manufacturers use electrolysis to coat the body parts in a layer of zinc. This protects the steel underneath from rust. This process is known as electroplating.

Chapter Four
Electricity and magnetism

Twenty-one years after Volta made the first battery, a Danish scientist called Hans Christian Ørsted found a link between electricity and magnetism.

Electromagnetism
Magnetism made by electricity is called electromagnetism. This force is the reason why many modern devices and machines, from lifts to electric motors, work.

Accidental discovery
Ørsted discovered electromagnetism by accident in 1820 while he was doing an experiment with some electrical equipment. Each time he turned on the equipment, a compass needle moved to line up with the wire. Ørsted worked out that the needle moved because electricity was flowing through wires in the equipment. The electricity made the wires act like magnets, which attracted the compass needle.

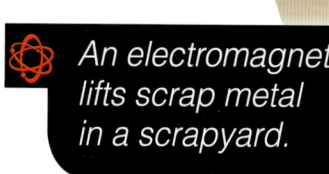
An electromagnet lifts scrap metal in a scrapyard.

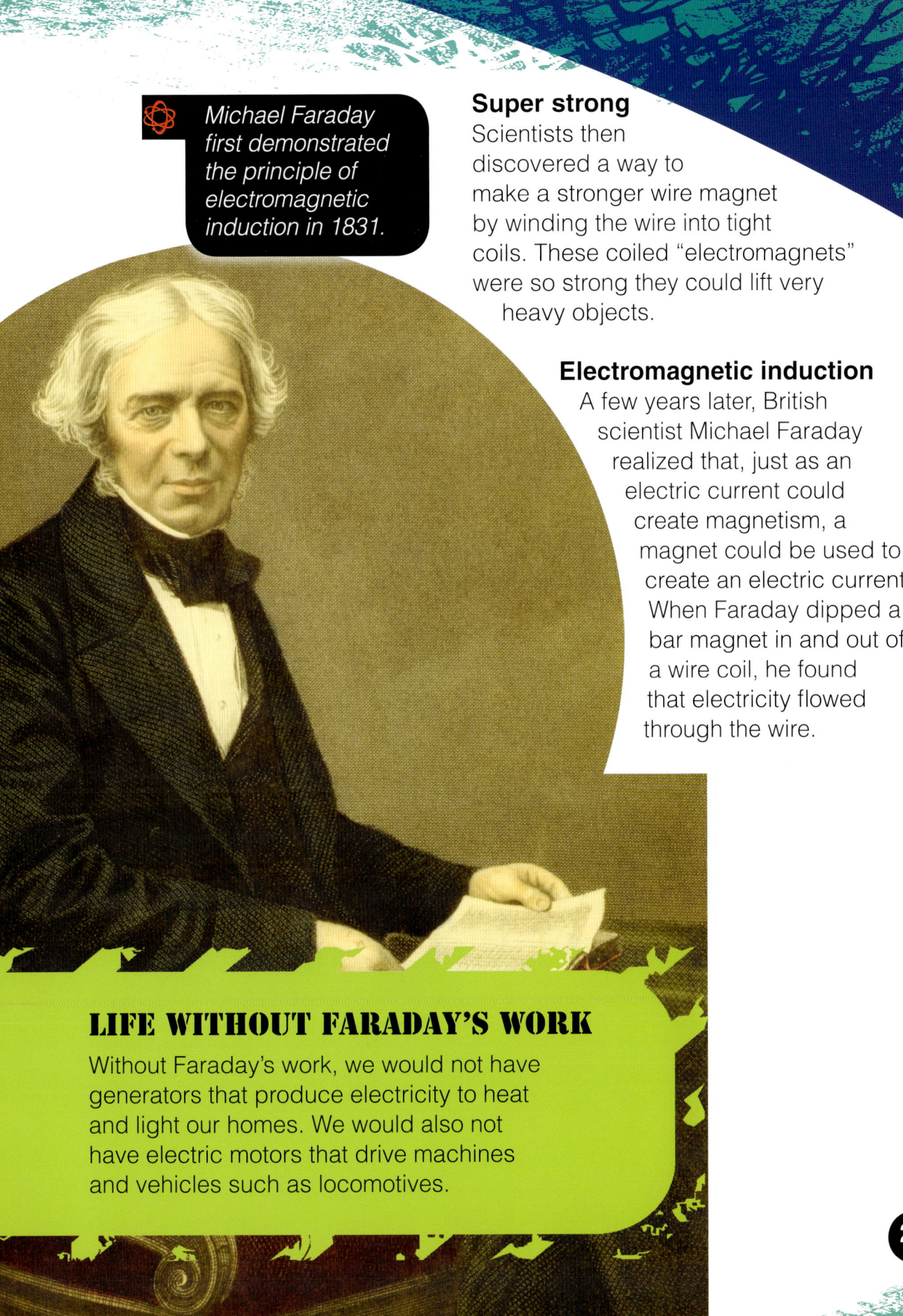

Michael Faraday first demonstrated the principle of electromagnetic induction in 1831.

Super strong
Scientists then discovered a way to make a stronger wire magnet by winding the wire into tight coils. These coiled "electromagnets" were so strong they could lift very heavy objects.

Electromagnetic induction
A few years later, British scientist Michael Faraday realized that, just as an electric current could create magnetism, a magnet could be used to create an electric current. When Faraday dipped a bar magnet in and out of a wire coil, he found that electricity flowed through the wire.

LIFE WITHOUT FARADAY'S WORK
Without Faraday's work, we would not have generators that produce electricity to heat and light our homes. We would also not have electric motors that drive machines and vehicles such as locomotives.

Generators

Generators are powerful machines that "generate" electricity from magnetism. The first generators were just small machines used to make tiny amounts of electricity. Later, engineers built giant generators to create electricity for whole cities.

The earliest generators were small machines used in laboratories to make electricity for scientific experiments.

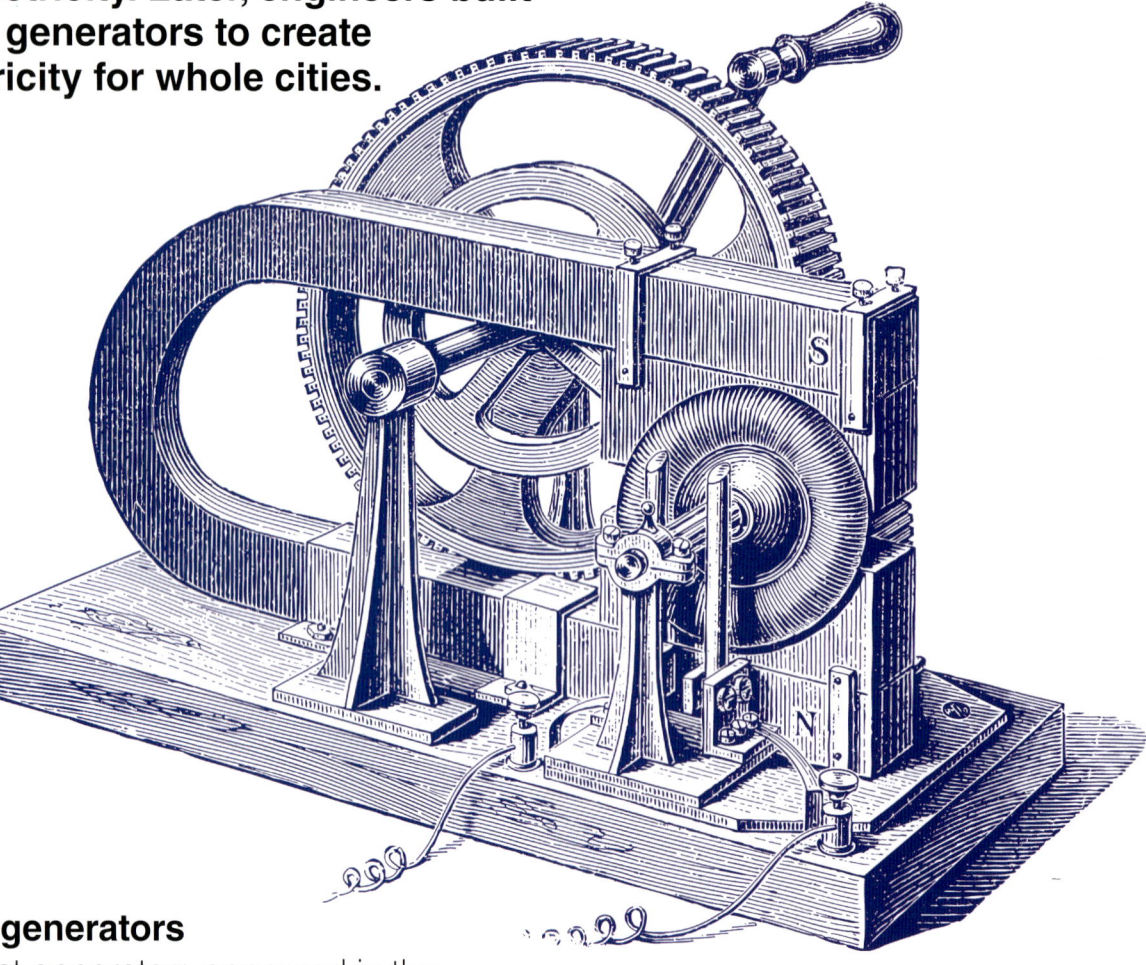

Early generators
The first generators appeared in the 1830s. They were called magneto-electric machines. Scientists used them to create electricity to carry out experiments in laboratories.

Most of these machines worked when a handle was turned, moving a wire coil between the poles of a magnet. As the wire cut through the magnetic field, an electric current flowed through the wire.

Dynamos

About ten years later, scientists replaced bar magnets with electromagnets to create a stronger magnetic field. These generators were called dynamos. They were used to make the arc lights that lit up lighthouses and street lights.

Power plants

The invention of the steam engine in the late 1800s had a big impact on the supply of electricity. Engineers used steam power to spin the blades of a steam turbine. In turn, the turbine turned wire coils through huge electromagnets, generating a lot of electricity. Modern generators still use steam to turn turbine blades, but fossil fuels or nuclear power heat the water to produce the steam.

SUPER SCIENCE FACT

Nuclear power comes from the energy locked inside atoms. Some atoms are unstable and break down into more stable atoms. When this happens, these atoms release a lot of energy. This energy is used to heat water and produce the steam needed to generate electricity.

The nuclear reactions taking place inside this power station release energy to heat water to create steam. The steam then drives turbines to generate electricity.

AC-DC

Generators produce two types of electricity: alternating current (AC) and direct current (DC). Alternating current changes direction many times every second. Direct current flows in the same direction all the time.

Alternators
When the wire coil of a generator cuts through a magnetic field, electricity flows through the wire. As the coil keeps turning, it cuts through the magnetic field in different directions. This results in a current that rises and falls. This electricity is called alternating current and generators are often called alternators.

The Tesla coil changes low-voltage electricity into an incredibly high voltage. When you touch the glass sphere, the electricity discharges as a bright spark.

Getting the electricity

Wires cannot be used to collect the electricity from the coil, because the coil constantly rotates and the wires would get tangled up. Instead, the generator has two metal rings, called slip rings, attached near each end of the coil. The slip rings make contact with the rotating coil through carbon brushes, which conduct the electricity away from it.

DC dynamos

Many machines work only with direct current. Instead of slip rings, DC dynamos use a switch called a commutator to change alternating current into direct current. The commutator works by switching the connection to the carbon brushes every half turn of the wire. As a result, the electric current always leaves the coil through one brush and back through the second brush.

> *Transformers increase the voltage of electricity generated by power stations. This prevents power loss as electricity passes through overhead power cables to homes.*

SUPER SCIENCE FACT

A transformer uses the alternating current in a wire coil to produce electricity in a second wire coil wound around the first coil. This is called an induction ring. By changing the number of turns in the second coil, scientists can increase or decrease the voltage of the electricity supply.

Electric motors

Electric motors use electricity to make things move. They are used to power many different machines, from lawnmowers and sewing machines to enormous pumps and vehicles such as ships.

The first motor

Michael Faraday built the first electric motor in 1821. He passed electricity through a simple wire and watched as it turned around the pole of a magnet. Although Faraday's motor was too simple to power a machine, it showed that electricity could one day be used to drive machines.

An electric motor works the bobbin and needle of this sewing machine. Isaac Singer invented the first electric sewing machine in 1850.

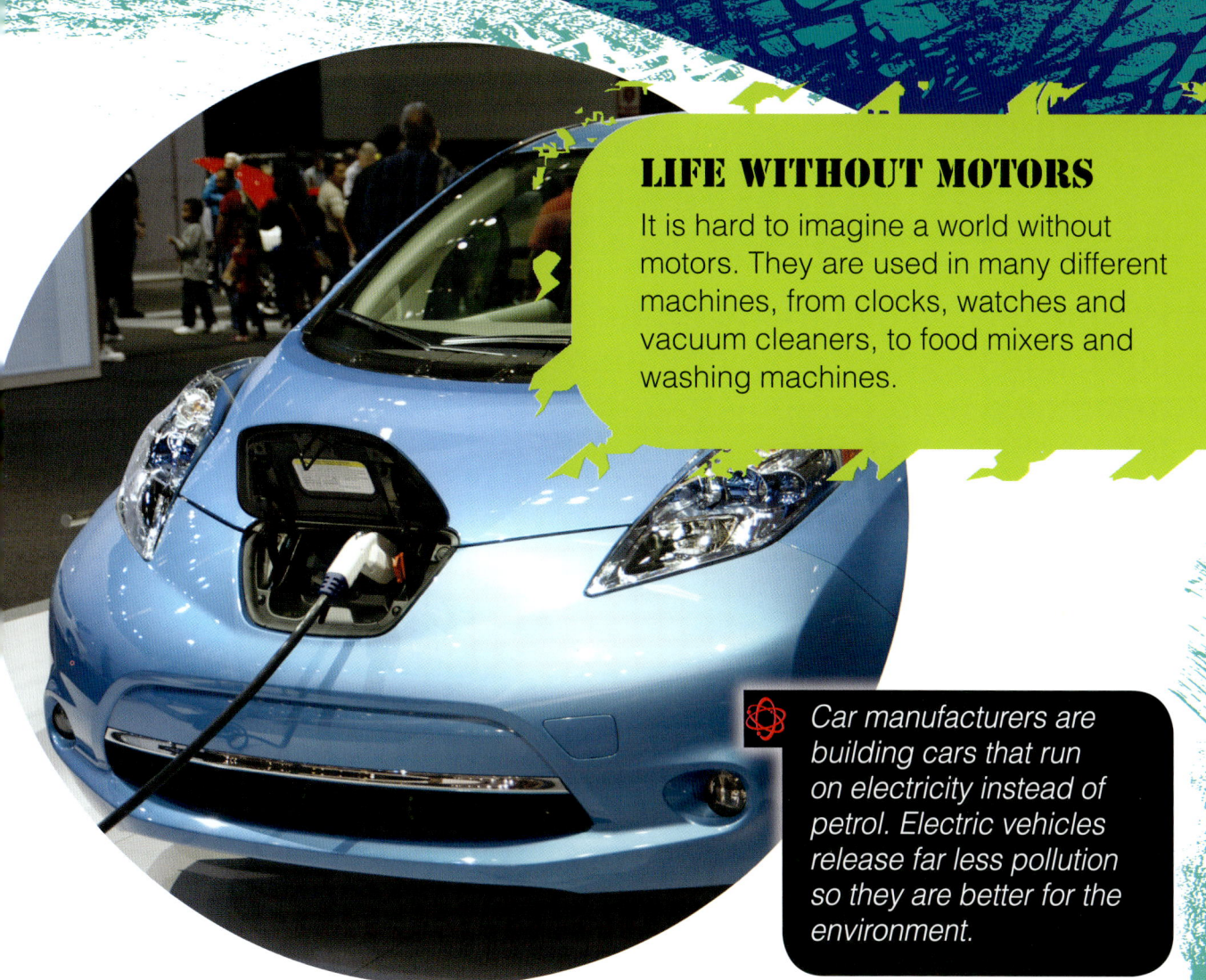

LIFE WITHOUT MOTORS

It is hard to imagine a world without motors. They are used in many different machines, from clocks, watches and vacuum cleaners, to food mixers and washing machines.

Car manufacturers are building cars that run on electricity instead of petrol. Electric vehicles release far less pollution so they are better for the environment.

Basic motors

Simple electric motors use direct current as a source of power. As electric current flows through a wire coil, it creates a magnetic field around the coil. As the coil sits between the poles of a magnet, it moves because magnets push against each other. This pushing force creates the turning power of the motor. Increasing the number of turns in the coil, as well as the number of coils themselves, increases the pushing force and therefore the power of the motor.

Modern motors

Most modern motors use alternating current as a source of power. These motors are called induction motors. They consist of a series of fixed electromagnets around a rotating steel core, which is called a rotor. The electromagnets create a magnetic field only when electricity flows through them. Switching the magnets on and off in turn changes the magnetic field around the rotor, forcing it to turn.

Chapter Five
Using electricity

People rely on electricity for heat and light, and to power many different machines, from computers and telephones to washing machines and televisions. Scientists and inventors are now looking for new ways to meet our never-ending demand for electric power.

People rely on electricity to power household appliances such as washing machines.

Electric power
Most of the world's electricity comes from burning fossil fuels, such as coal and gas, in power stations. Overhead power lines carry this electricity from power stations to houses, factories and offices.

Early power stations

An American inventor called Thomas Edison designed and built the world's first power station in New York, USA. It opened in 1882 and supplied electricity to a few buildings in New York City. In just a few years, a network of power stations and overhead cables, called a power grid, had spread across cities in the United States – and the rest of the world. For the first time, people could light and heat a room at the flick of a switch.

Modern power stations

Most modern power stations create electricity by burning fossil fuels. Burning the fuel creates the heat to boil water and create steam. The steam turns huge turbines to power generators. The problem with fossil fuels is that they create pollution, and they will eventually run out.

This hydroelectric power station channels water from a reservoir just behind the dam through turbines. As the turbines rotate, they generate electricity.

SUPER SCIENCE FACT

In the UK, about 1.8 per cent of all electricity is made in hydroelectric power stations. They generate electricity by channelling the water from rivers through huge turbines, which power the generators.

Electric machines

When electricity became available in people's homes, its main use was for lighting. Today, electricity makes most of our appliances work.

⚛ *One of the earliest uses of electricity was for communication. The telegraph sent messages along wires as pulses of electricity.*

New designs
The earliest electric machines relied on electricity to make heat. Inventors designed appliances such as the electric iron to smooth out creases from clothes. The electric motor led to new inventions to make life easier, such as food mixers and vacuum cleaners. These machines were expensive, so only rich people could afford them.

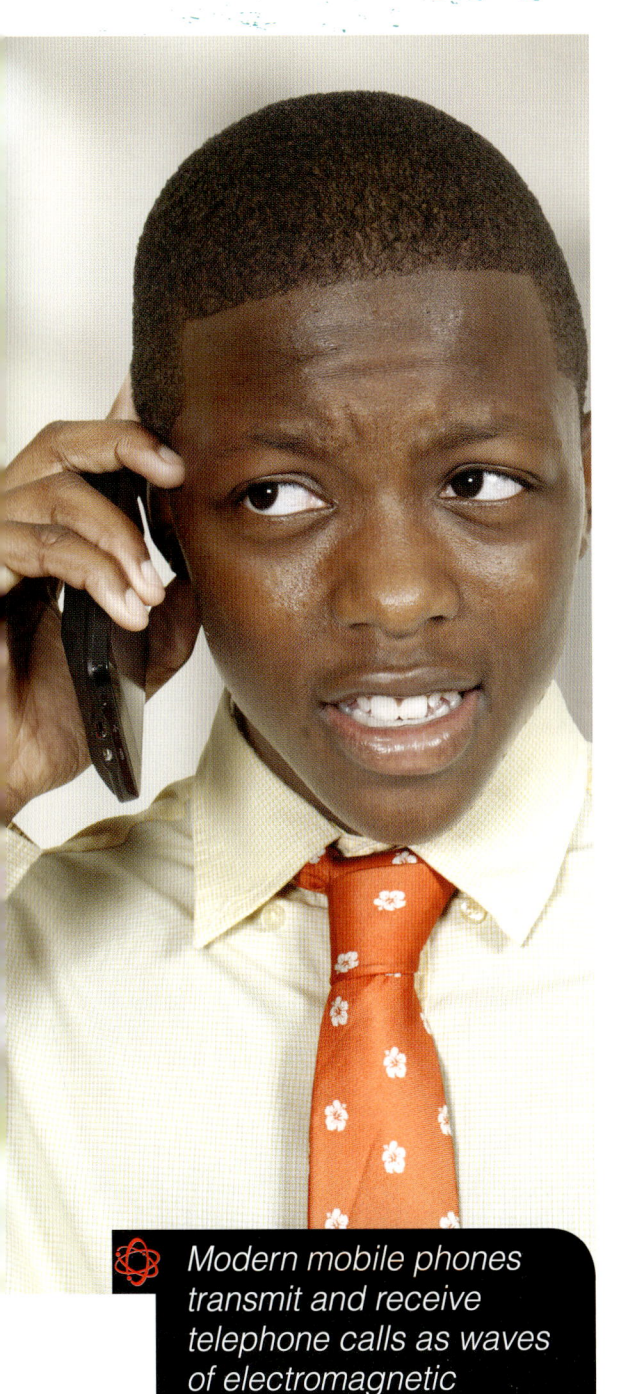

Electric communication

Telegraph operators sent messages in Morse code. The code is a series of dots and dashes created by tiny pulses, which represent letters and numbers. Several inventors took this idea further. They built machines that changed speech into electrical signals and sent them along wires. They were the first telephones.

Wireless communication

In the late 1800s, a British scientist called James Clerk Maxwell found a new link between electricity and magnetism. He showed that energy travelled in waves of electromagnetic radiation. These waves travelled through the air and could be used to send signals without wires. This led to the invention of the radio to send sound messages, and later the television to send images, through the airwaves.

Modern mobile phones transmit and receive telephone calls as waves of electromagnetic radiation that travel through the air.

SUPER SCIENCE FACT

Many people credit the invention of the telephone to the British inventor Alexander Graham Bell in 1875. In fact, an Italian-American inventor called Antonio Meucci had invented a similar device more than 20 years earlier. Meucci did not register his invention, however, so his role has since often been overlooked.

The computer age

The computer is one of the most important inventions of the twentieth century. People use computers all the time – for playing games and music, sending emails, and shopping on the internet. Computers also control many other machines, from cars and mobile phones to wristwatches.

Early computers

The very first computers worked without electricity. The abacus was a simple computer. It was invented in ancient Egypt around 2,500 years ago. It used strings and beads to add and subtract numbers by hand. In the 1800s, the British mathematician Charles Babbage designed a steam-powered computer called the Analytical Engine. He never built his computer, but the idea was a machine that performed calculations by using information on punched cards.

The abacus was the first computer used to perform simple maths.

Electronic computers

Modern computers work using electric currents that flow through switches. The switch turns the electric current on and off. Computers read the on-and-off signals as a set of instructions to do different tasks. At first, the switches were giant glass tubes called vacuum tubes.

Using switches

Early electronic computers were huge and used lots of electricity. Later, scientists invented much smaller switches, called transistors, to replace the vacuum tubes. Today's computers use wafer-thin slices of silicon to control the electric current. These silicon chips are no bigger than your fingernail and contain millions of transistors to control the current.

The on-and-off pulses of electricity that flow through the circuits of a modern computer allow you to play games, listen to music and use the internet.

LIFE WITHOUT COMPUTERS

It is hard to imagine a world without computers. They are all around us and hidden away inside many different machines. In fact, it is thought that many people use about 150 computers every day – sometimes without even knowing it.

New sources

Most of our electricity comes from burning fossil fuels, which pollute the environment. The challenge for today's scientists is to find new ways to make electricity without burning fossil fuels.

Problems with fossil fuels

Fossil fuels are the remains of animals and plants that lived millions of years ago. Over time, their bodies break down under the ground and turn into coal, oil and natural gas. The problem is that we are using these fuels faster than they are being created, so they will eventually run out. Fossil fuels also create a lot of pollution. When they burn, fossil fuels give off carbon dioxide. This gas pollutes the air and creates acid rain and global warming.

The solar panels on the roof of this house absorb energy from the sun and convert it into electricity.

SUPER SCIENCE FACT

Solar and wind power are renewable energy sources. Unlike fossil fuels, renewable energy sources will never run out. Other renewable energy sources include hydropower and geothermal power. Hydropower uses the energy from flowing water to create electricity. Geothermal power uses natural sources of heat inside Earth to produce electricity.

Most power stations burn fossil fuels to make electricity. Fossil fuels are in limited supply and pollute the environment, so scientists are now developing renewable energy sources such as solar power.

Solar power
Scientists are now developing new ways to make electricity. One of these is to collect the energy from sunlight using solar panels and change it into electrical energy. The panels contain cells that generate electricity when light shines on them.

Wind power
Another way to make electricity is by harnessing the power of the wind. Scientists have built machines called wind turbines. The blades of the turbine spin when the wind blows over them. This turns a small generator to make electricity.

The future of electricity

Electricity has been around since the beginning of the universe. But it has only been in the last 150 years that scientists and inventors have harnessed electric power. The science of electricity is still very young. Who knows what the future holds for this amazing energy source?

The next time you turn on the television to watch your favourite programme, think about how much you rely on electricity.

From light bulbs to machines
When Thomas Edison built the first power station in 1882, one of the main uses of electricity was power for light bulbs. Over time, scientists harnessed the power of electricity for more and more machines. Today, electric machines are all around us. Inventors are still coming up with new ideas, such as electric clothes and shoes, to provide us with constant power.

Wireless electricity

We use wireless technology when we watch television and connect to the internet. Scientists are now working on ways to power machines using "wireless electricity". They plan to transmit electricity as waves of electromagnetic radiation. The problem is making this wireless electricity both safe and efficient to use.

Saving electricity

Many countries are investing a lot of money in renewable energy sources such as solar power. Many people feel this money might be better spent finding ways to save electricity. Everyone needs to reduce the amount of electricity they use by turning off lights, computers and other machines when they are not in use.

SUPER SCIENCE FACT

The United States is one of the world's biggest energy consumers. Americans make up less than 5 per cent of the world population, but they use more than 25 per cent of the world's electricity supply.

Although electricity lights up our lives and provides the power for countless machines and vehicles, we rarely stop to think about it.

Glossary

acid rain any form of precipitation (rain, hail or snow) that is acidic. Acid rain damages trees and pollutes water in dams and rivers.

atoms tiny particles that make up everything in the universe

battery source of electricity consisting of one or more electric cells

cells (electric) simple electricity-generating unit of a battery

circuit unbroken pathway through which electricity flows

compound chemical substance that is made up of two or more elements

conductor substance that lets electricity flow through it easily

current flow of electrons through a conducting material

electrode conductor that makes contact with the non-metallic part of an electric circuit

electrolyte liquid or paste that conducts electricity

electromagnet magnet created by the flow of electricity through a wire coil

electromagnetic radiation energy that flows through space as particles and waves

electron tiny particle found inside an atom. Electrons carry negative electrical charge.

fossil fuels coal, oil and natural gas made from the remains of animals and plants that lived millions of years ago

friction force that acts in the opposite direction to movement

generator machine that converts movement into electricity

global warming gradual rise in the average temperature of Earth's atmosphere. Scientists believe that this rise in temperature is responsible for climate change.

insulator substance that does not allow electricity to flow through it easily

molecules combinations of two or more atoms

motor machine that converts electricity into movement

nerves fibres that pass electrical signals through the body

radio form of electromagnetic radiation with a very long wavelength

resistor substance that resists the flow of electricity through it

silicon chip tiny piece of silicon that contains millions of transistors and other electronic components. Silicon chips control computers.

solar power electricity that comes from harnessing the Sun's energy

static electricity electricity that builds up on objects when they rub against each other

telegraph machine that transmits signals along wires as pulses of electricity

transformer device that increases or decreases the voltage in an electric circuit

turbine machine with blades that spins to create electricity in a generator

voltage driving force that pushes electrons around an electric circuit

Find out more

Books

DK Findout! Energy, Emily Dodd (DK Children, 2018)

Electricity (Essential Physical Science), Louise and Richard Spilsbury (Raintree, 2014)

Electricity (Flowchart Science), Louise Spilsbury (Raintree, 2018)

From Falling Water to Electric Car: An energy journey through the world of electricity, Ian Graham (Raintree, 2016)

Websites

www.bbc.com/bitesize/articles/zxv482p
Learn more about conductors and insulators.

www.dkfindout.com/uk/science/electricity/
Find out more about electricity.

Index

atoms 12, 16, 17, 22, 23, 24, 25, 31

Babbage, Charles 40
batteries 14, 18, 19, 20, 21, 22, 23, 26, 28
Bell, Alexander Graham 39

commutators 33
computers 5, 11, 36, 40–41, 45
conductors 22, 23, 24

Daniell, John Frederic 20
Davy, Humphry 27
dynamos 31, 33

Edison, Thomas 37, 44
electric cells 20–21
electric current 17, 18, 19, 23, 24, 25, 26, 29, 30, 32, 33, 35, 41
electric lights 10, 31, 38, 44, 45
electric motors 28, 29, 34–35, 38
electrodes 20, 21, 23, 26, 27
electrolysis 26–27
electrolyte 20, 21
electromagnetic radiation 39, 45
electromagnetism 28, 29
electrons 16, 17, 19, 22, 23, 24, 25

energy 4, 5, 6, 10, 15, 17, 23, 31, 39, 43, 44, 45
engines 11, 31

Faraday, Michael 29, 34
fossil fuels 31, 36, 37, 42, 43
Franklin, Benjamin 13

Galvani, Luigi 18, 19
generators 28, 29, 30, 31, 32, 33, 37, 43
geothermal power 43

heat 5, 6, 7, 8, 10, 29, 31, 36, 37, 38, 43
hydroelectricity 37

insulators 22–23

Leclanché, Georges 21
light 5, 6, 7, 8, 10, 29, 31, 36, 37, 38, 43, 45
lightning 4, 6, 7, 13, 14

magnetism 28, 29, 30, 39
Maxwell, James Clerk 39
metals 13, 14, 15, 18, 19, 20, 23, 24, 25, 27, 33
Meucci, Antonio 39
mobile phones 11, 21, 39, 40
molecules 26

neutrons 16, 17
Nicholson, William 26
nuclear power 31

Ohm, Georg 24, 25
Ørsted, Hans Christian 28

power stations 28, 31, 36, 37, 44
protons 16, 17

resistors 24–25

solar power 43, 45
static electricity 7, 17

transformers 33
transistors 41
turbines 31, 37, 43

vacuum tubes 41
Van de Graaff, Robert 15
Volta, Alessandro 19, 20, 26, 28
Voltaic pile 19, 20, 26
voltage 23, 24, 25, 33

Wimshurst, James 14
wind power 43